Brian Moore's
Football Quiz Book

Brian Moore

Illustrated by
Gary Rees

Jointly published by
INDEPENDENT TELEVISION BOOKS LTD
247 Tottenham Court Road, London W1P 0AU

and

ARROW BOOKS LTD
3 Fitzroy Square, London W1

An imprint of the Hutchinson Publishing Group

London Melbourne Sydney Auckland
Wellington Johannesburg and agencies
throughout the world

First published 1977
© Brian Moore 1977

ISBN 0 09 915540 0

**Made and printed in Great Britain
by The Anchor Press Ltd
Tiptree, Essex**

The Publishers wish to thank all the football clubs for
the use of their badges.

Contents

Introduction   5

Players   7
World stars   8
Who am I?   9
The name's the same   10
Families   15
The letters game in England   16
The letters game in Scotland, Wales,
     Northern Ireland and Eire   18
The hot shots   20
Players' names and places   21

Teams   22
The final tables   23
Grounds   24
Badges   26
The 1976-7 season   28
The Third Division   29
The Fourth Division   31
Nicknames   32
Grounds mix and match   33
Club quiz   34

International Football   37
World stars on the move   38
Famous teams   39
Scotland   42
Wales and Ireland   43
A geography lesson   45
Europe   46
European cups   47
World Cup   49

Mixed Bag 51

Mixed bag 52

True or false 53

For the experts 55

Penalties 55

Free for all 56

Football history 57

Rules of the game 59

Soccer dates 60

Some early dates 60

So you think you're an expert? 61

Pot pourri—1 63

Pot pourri—2 64

Pot pourri—3 65

Referee's Decisions 67

Match Reports 71

Answers 76

Introduction

My earliest fascination with football quizzes came in the schoolroom during particularly dreary, to me at any rate, Latin and maths lessons. Slips of paper passed to a neighbour seeking the names of the Manchester United Cup winning team of 1948 and the goalscorers—and the sight of him struggling to remember them—at least made the clock move round a little faster.

Through the years my love of compiling baffling football questions has never diminished. It has seen me through guard duty during National Service; through long train journeys to matches and short crowded ones to work; through idle moments round a holiday pool; and less frantic moments in the *World of Sport* office.

My greatest adversary was always Johnny Haynes, that marvellous captain of Fulham and England. Whenever we met over the years we always substituted any formal greetings by: 'I've got a good one for you this time!' And we'd spend the next hour or so dragging our memories back over the years for questions and answers and getting a lot of fun from it all.

Now, with wonderful collaboration from Chris Rhys, we have the *Brian Moore's Football Quiz Book*. I hope you will agree that it is more adventurous than most football quiz books. Indeed, our aim has been to make it a fun book and one that does not rely on stifling hours of devotion to the record books.

All you need is an average knowledge of the game of football and of the people who play it. And most of the time you'll find that you need to go no further back than seven or eight years, as we set you questions about players and games that you would either have seen yourself or read about in your favourite football magazine.

Mind you, there are some questions that offer an enormous challenge. If you fancy your chances—turn to the section For the Experts. If you take a particular interest in overseas football— you also are not forgotten. If you watch your football in Scotland or in the lower Divisions—you'll find something to tackle. And if you enjoy tangling with the laws of the game, Reg Paine, the refereeing expert at the Football Association, has kindly offered a few head-scratching situations for you.

You may find that in one or two of these questions the answer has been made incorrect because a player has moved to another club. Please accept our apologies and try to bear in mind that the questions were put together during the summer of 1977.

So now get to work. Find a football-mad friend and make your football quizzes competitive. Certainly you'll need a little knowledge—but by good use of this book you can also learn so much about the game. But above all we want you to have fun!

Brian Moore

Players

'The game is about players.' That is something you often hear today when football sometimes seems in danger of being overtaken by politics, money and power. So what better than to start my quiz book with a chapter on players? How well do you know them? Test your knowledge here as we try all sorts of tricks on you!

I particularly like the section on families and the matching of a player's name with a town. We've tried to get a nice balance here that will test your wits and powers of deduction, along with a series—like the World Stars—where you really have to possess pure football knowledge.

Some of the questions will be very difficult for you—but I'm sure that's the way you want it!

Brian Moore

World stars

Can you match these players with their clubs?

1	Berti Vogts	Zurich
2	Hans Krankl	Stal Mielec
3	Christian Piot	St Etienne
4	Jan Peters	Flamengo
5	Hugo Gatti	Ferencvaros
6	Zico	Borussia Munchen Gladbach
7	Franz Beckenbauer	Barcelona
8	Pirri	Rapid Vienna
9	Ralf Edstroem	Dynamo Kiev
10	Sepp Maier	Standard Liege
11	Marian Masny	Juventus
12	Dominique Rocheteau	Boca Juniors
13	Jurgen Croy	NEC Nijmigen
14	Dimitros Papaioannou	Sachsenring Zwickau
15	Gregoriz Lato	Real Madrid
16	Dino Zoff	New York Cosmos
17	Johan Cruyff	Bayern Munich
18	Rene Botteron	PSV Eindhoven
19	Oleg Blokhine	AEK Athens
20	Laszlo Balint	Slovan Bratislava

Answers on page 76

Who am I?

1 I started my career with Wrexham, and played 42 League games before being transferred to Arsenal at the age of 20. I played only 16 times for them, before returning to Wrexham. I made my international debut in 1970-1 and was a regular member of the International team from 1974 to 1976 (when I was way past 30) winning 13 caps. When my boss left to join Middlesbrough, I became manager of the club for which I originally played. Who am I?

2 I was born in 1941. My first club was Chesterfield, and I also trained as a teacher at Loughborough College. I came south and signed for a club with whom I was to win the 'Double'. When the qualification laws changed I played for Scotland on two occasions in 1971-2, once against Holland and once against Portugal. When I retired I went into television and now host the programme *Football Focus*. Who am I?

3 I played for the majority of my career with Fulham, for whom I was an inside forward. I was the first player to really put forward the needs of the professional footballer, and I was instrumental in having the £20 per week wage abolished. I was manager of Coventry City, and again helped bring the game forward as family entertainment. I am involved in the game in Saudi Arabia, and work on television. Who am I?

4 I was one of the survivors of a terrible air crash. I became a first team regular shortly afterwards and played for my club, Manchester United, for nearly 20 years. I then went to Preston North End and had a brief spell as manager. I scored a record number of goals for England and I was the second Englishman to reach the target of 100 caps. My international career finished after the 1970 World Cup. Who am I?

5 I began my career with Blackpool and I played my first match for England in 1964-5, and gained my first 14 caps at Blackpool. After my performance in the 1966 World Cup I was transferred to Everton for a fee of £110,000. I stayed there some six seasons before joining Arsenal for £220,000. I was the first England captain under Don Revie, and I gained 72 caps before joining Southampton in 1976. Who am I?

6 I began my career as a halfback with Celtic. I then moved south of the border and played for Preston, with whom I gained the first of my 25 caps in 1951-2. After a spell with Arsenal I went into management and led Chelsea to the 1967 Cup Final. After leaving Chelsea I went to a host of places, QPR, Aston Villa, Rotherham and even Oporto in Portugal. On my return I went to Hull, then was manager of Scotland. I also used to be the manager of one of England's most famous clubs. Who am I?

Answers on page 76

The name's the same

1 All the following footballers have the same surname as other famous sportsmen from other sports. Can you name them?

a) A Burnley striker of a couple of years ago, and a famous US golfer

b) An Ipswich player and our best known heavyweight boxer

c) A Birmingham City defender whose surname is pronounced the same as one of our Ryder Cup golfers

d) Lord Hesketh's new number 1 racing driver and an established England International

e) A Fulham forward in the 1976-7 season and an Australian wicketkeeper who have identical names

f) Both stop the ball—a recent England keeper and a former Sussex and England wicketkeeper

g) An English International striker who has the same surname as a cricketer who wrecked England's bowling in the series against the West Indies in 1976

h) One of the world's most famous boxers of the 1920s has the same surname as one of Chelsea's centre backs

i) A Midland Second Division keeper has the same surname as a famous wrestler

j) A Sheffield United striker has the same surname as one of Rugby Union's all time greats

2 Who are these players who share their surnames with motor cars?

a) Luton Town's winger

b) Mansfield Town's player-manager

c) He went from Ipswich to Plymouth Argyle in 1976-7

d) Southend player who may come from a nearby factory

e) A Blackpool fullback

3 There are even a number of players who share their names with birds. Can you name the following?

a) A Bournemouth player often in the first team in 1976

b) A Charlton Athletic player who set a League record

c) Chelsea's new fullback who helped in the 1976-7 promotion campaign

d) Doncaster Rovers' goalkeeper

e) Grimsby Town's striker

f) Another keeper, he plays for Huddersfield Town

g) An Oldham Athletic midfield player

h) Scunthorpe United defender, and the third of this name in this section

i) York City's former striker

4 There are some footballers whose names have appeared regularly on the TV screen. Can you name the following?

a) Name two players (one in the First, one in the Second Division) who might be stars of two different TV detective series. Another clue: their surnames are the same as the titles of the programmes

b) A Fulham International player is the first half of an old, long running TV series. The second half is the word 'Place'. Who is the footballer?

c) Which two well-known footballers can be found in the title of two Saturday TV soccer programmes?

d) Who is the Rotherham player who could be one of Great Uncle Bulgaria's relations?

5 In which teams would you find a Lord, an Earl(e), a Queen, a King, a Prince, a Bar(r)on, and a Knight?

6 Now try to identify players whose names make you feel hungry!

   a) If you're out for a late meal, you might find an Irish and English International in an Indian restaurant. Who are they?

   b) Managers looking for a bargain buy would find the following in a greengrocers—a star of the 1976 Cup Final, an English International and a Cardiff City player. Can you name them?

   c) A fishmonger even if he can't spell properly can provide an International keeper, a West Ham reserve and a fine Stoke City forward. Can you name them?

7 Here is a clue to the identity of the following players—each shares his surname with a different type of worker. Who are they?

   a) He came to Ipswich from Plymouth

   b) A QPR youngster who often commands a midfield place

   c) A West Country First Division defender

   d) Tottenham's central defender or fullback

   e) Luton's goalkeeper

   f) International defenders: one of whom is with Bristol City, the other with Ipswich Town

   g) An England International and his brothers originally from Walsall, and a man who has scored over 200 League goals for Newport County, Cardiff City and Bristol City

   h) Bradford City's 20 goal striker and Colchester United's fullback

i) Bournemouth's goalkeeper

j) The former Ipswich player now with Mansfield, Barnsley's inside forward and Bournemouth's centre back all share the same surname—who are they?

k) Middlesbrough's International fullback

l) Another keeper, he's with Southampton

m) Yet another keeper, he's with Swansea City

n) Blackpool's defender

o) One of Brighton's best defenders, and a former Hereford star

p) Joe, of Aldershot, a defender. and Geoff of Bournemouth

q) One of Colchester's promotion side, a midfield player

r) Two south coast defenders with different 1976-7 Third Division sides, one being promoted

s) Former Crystal Palace and Coventry City goalkeeper

t) Bill, of Chelsea, and Paul of the England Under-21's and Sheffield United

u) Derek, a Chester player for many seasons

v) Former Stoke City keeper, now, in 1977, at Northwich Victoria

Answers on page 77

Families

Many fathers and sons, brothers, uncles and cousins have played for the same football teams. Below are some of the more recent examples—how many can you guess?

1 Who are the brothers on Chelsea's books?

2 Which father picked his son for his First Division debut in 1976-7?

3 Which brothers played for Luton Town in the early 1970s?

4 Which cousins were in the 1977 Welsh International team?

5 Which brother joined his younger brother in the same 1976 First Division line-up?

6 Which brothers played in the 1976 European Cup Final?

7 Who are the brothers, one of whom played fullback for England in 1968 and the other was an Under-23 International in the 1970s who has since retired?

8 Who were the twins who played for Holland in 1976-7?

9 Name the brothers, one of whom has played for England, and the other who has kept goal for Wales?

10 Can you name the brothers who played in the 1967 FA Cup Final?

11 Which brothers played in the European Cup Final in Paris in 1975?

12 Name the Third Division keeper in the 1976-7 season whose elder brother gained 21 caps for Wales up to 1972, also as a goalkeeper.

13 Can you name two brothers who are in the Football League and another brother who plays in the Scottish League?

14 Who are the twins who came south from Chester in 1974?

15 Which First Division manager picked his own son for his Football League debut in 1975?

16 Who are Ken and Terry of recent First Division fame?

17 What is the surname of Barry and Colin, two of Mansfield's promotion side?

18 Which brothers played 141 times for England?

19 Who were the brothers who played cricket for Middlesex and soccer for Arsenal since the war?

20 Which Football League goalkeeper has a brother who won a bronze medal at the Olympic Games in the 400 metres hurdles?

21 Who are the two brothers with a South London club, one of whom has been very unlucky with injuries?

22 A young Middlesex cricketer and his brother on Arsenal's books?

Answers on page 78

The letters game in England

Many players represented England during the years 1969-70 to 1976. Can you name the following—using their initials as a clue? There may be more as time goes on.

1 Name the only footballer to have played for England whose surname begins with the letter V.

2 Five players whose surnames begin with R have worn the England jersey. Which two have both played for the same club?

3 Which three defenders, whose surnames begin with N, represented England during the period 1970 to 1976?

4 Which two centre forwards, whose surnames begin with the letter J, played for England between 1970 and 1976?

5 Which two northern players, whose surnames begin with D, have represented England since 1970?

6 Only one player, whose surname begins with A, has represented England during the 1970-6 period. Who is he?

7 Name the two players, whose surnames begin with S, who have gained just one cap for England between 1970 and 1976—one has a double-barrelled name.

8 Two players, with the same surname which begins with T, have played for England since 1970. They are not brothers. Who are they? And a further clue, they both played for the same club.

9 Similarly, two players, with the same surname which begins with F, have played for England since 1970. They, also, are not brothers. Who are they?

10 Who gained his only cap for England in 1971? His surname begins with the letter H.

11 Name five English Internationals who have played for London clubs since 1970 whose names all begin with the letter B.

12 Two players beginning with the letter G gained their first caps for England in 1976-7. Who are they?

13 There have been three England fullbacks who have played for England since 1970 whose surnames begin with the letter L. Who are the two who played for the same club? Can you name the other player as well?

14 Who are the five English Internationals of the last 10 years whose surnames start with the letters Hu?

15 Who are the three wingers to have played for England since 1974 whose surnames start with the letter T?

16 Think carefully before answering. How many English

Internationals whose surnames begin with the letter E have played for their country within the last six years?

17 Four players beginning with the letter P have played for England since 1970. Who are they?

18 In the 1974 seasons, who were the three players from the same Midland club who played for England and whose surnames begin with W?

19 Who are the two players (from the same club) whose names begin with the letter K who wore the England jersey in 1977?

20 Who are the two England centre forwards since 1975 whose names begin with the letter M?

Answers on page 78

The letters game in Scotland, Wales, Northern Ireland and Eire

One general clue. All the players below are Internationals.

1 These International players, all beginning with the letter B, played for Scotland, Wales, Northern Ireland or Eire between 1970 and 1976. Can you name them?

a) A Scot who played for Norwich City
b) A Scottish keeper with Sheffield United
c) Birmingham City's utility Scot
d) The most famous Irishman of all
e) An Irishman at Oldham Athletic

2   Now the letter R

a) A player who earned 39 Welsh caps from 1965 to 1972
b) His namesake, though the name is spelt differently, plays the same position as (a), from Sheffield United and Cardiff
c) Three 'Roberts' have played since 1971. Christian names and clubs please
d) Scotland's 1976-7 keeper
e) One of Gillingham's rare Internationals, he played for Eire in 1973

3   The letter S

a) Middlesbrough's midfield Scot
b) A Scot who gained the last of his 21 caps when he was with Coventry City
c) This Welshman began at Wrexham and went to Everton
d) Irish Pat, who is on Ipswich's transfer list
e) A Welsh keeper from 1964 to 1975

4   And finally, the letter C

a) A man of Eire, who plays for Fortuna Cologne in West Germany
b) Another player from Eire, he was at Fulham between 1964 and 1976
c) Scottish Eddie from Sheffield United
d) Chelsea's Scottish star from 1968 to 1975
e) Coventry City's midfield Welshman, transferred to Wrexham

Answers on page 79

The hot shots

1 Who was the First Division top scorer in 1972-3 with a London club?

2 Who was a north-east club player, who led the Second. Division lists, with 24 goals in 1967-8, 24 in 1969-70 and 25 in 1970-1?

3 Who was a 26-goal Midland Second Division striker, top of the Division charts in 1973-4?

4 Who was top of the First Division lists in 1971-2, when he played with Manchester City?

5 Who led the Fourth Division scorers with 42 in 1970-1, then notched 35 the following year in the Third Division?

6 Who was transferred to West Ham after scoring 26 goals for Watford in 1973-4 in the Third Division?

7 Whose 20 Second Division goals in 1974-5 helped Aston Villa into the First Division?

8 Who scored 34 League goals for Walsall in 1975-6?

9 Who finished with 44 goals during his spell as a player for England?

10 Who topped the Scottish League lists in 1975-6 —Dalglish, Pettigrew, Parlane or Gray?

11 Who was the last player to score five goals in a First Division match? He achieved the feat against Luton Town in 1975.

12 In the Second Division, which player, now a well-known manager, scored 121 goals in three successive seasons (from 1958 to 1960)? He was the Division's top scorer in all those three years.

13 Who was the Fourth Division player who acheived the rare feat of scoring four goals in a match three times during the 1975-6 season?

14 Which player has scored more League goals than any other current (1976-7) First Division player?

Answers on page 79

Players' names and places

If you are going on a long journey by train, or by car, you can pass the time by thinking up players' names which are the same as those of towns, villages, counties or even countries. Try to guess some of the following; if you're having difficulty look up the team lists in the paper before you check your answers.

1 A London club captain who may come from Berkshire.

2 A Midland utility player more at home in the north-east.

3 A Midland goalkeeper whose name (mis-spelt) is a place in Lancashire.

4 A north-east fullback who comes from the same place as question number 3.

5 A Midland player who comes from a neighbouring Yorkshire city.

6 He plays for Oxford, but could come from a brewery town.

7 Does Chico come from Scotland's Douglas Park team?

8 Hereford's Kevin could keep goal in a London suburb

9 Swindon's Kenny could live up the road in the next county.

10 A Torquay defender who could be the third from this Lancashire town.

11 Which Southampton player's name is the same as that of a Somerset city?

12 Name two First Division players with surnames which are also countries.

13 Which London club footballer's surname is the same as an English county?

14 Which Arsenal footballer has the same surname as a Scottish county?

Answers on page 80

Teams

This is a general chapter where—as well as your memory—we are testing your overall knowledge of League clubs . . . their nicknames, the names of grounds as well as the history of certain clubs.

How good is your memory of last year's season? It's amazing how hard it is sometimes to remember the things that seemed so important only a few months earlier. See how you cope as you try to brush up your memory of 1976-7.

Why not bring in the competitive spirit here—and with a friend take alternate questions in the sections dealing with last season and allow 10 seconds for every answer. Quick-fire fun—with two points for a correct answer and one point for a good try.

Brian Moore

The final tables

Although the new season is now upon us, how many of these facts and figures from last season can you still remember?

1 Which club scored more goals than anyone else in the four Divisions?

2 Which club was unbeaten at home in their 21 Second Division League matches?

3 Which club picked up the least number of points of all 92 League clubs?

4 Only one club in the Third Division was unbeaten at home in League matches. Which one?

5 Which League club won only three League matches all season?

6 Which was the only club not to record an away win in the First Division in 1976-7?

7 Which Fourth Division club was unbeaten at home in League matches?

8 Which two Fourth Division clubs failed to record an away win in their League programme?

9 Which was the only club to concede 100 League goals?

10 Which city provided two promoted clubs?

Answers on page 80

Grounds

Some football grounds are as famous as the teams which play there. Are you familiar with their names?

1 Which six clubs, all of whom played in the First Division in 1976-7, have 'Park' in the names of their home grounds?

2 Which Football League club plays its home matches at a ground with the same name as that of Newcastle United? And which club at a ground with the same name as that of Stoke City?

3 Which Football League club shares its home ground with a County Cricket club?

4 Which two clubs, who played in the lower two Divisions in 1976-7, play their home matches on Recreation Grounds?

5 Which three clubs in the Football League play their home matches on grounds whose names end in 'Moor'?

6 Which 1976-7 First Division club has the smallest ground (measured in terms of having the smallest record attendance)?

7 Which English First Division club plays its home matches on a ground whose name contains that of another sport?

8 Which two clubs play their home matches at grounds with 'Meadow' in their names?

9 Which 1976-7 First Division club has the largest ground (measured in terms of having the largest record attendance)?

10 Which Football League ground overlooks the Oxford/Cambridge Boat Race course?

11 Which three club grounds have the names of trees in their titles?

12 Which ground has in its title the name of an imaginary creature which was supposed to have the head and wings of an eagle and the body of a lion?

13 Name two Football League club grounds with the word 'Valley' in their titles?

14 Which Football League ground has the same name as that of a famous Speedway club?

15 Four grounds, belonging to teams that in 1977 were in the lower Divisions, have names to do with religion. Which four are they? (This question doesn't include names of saints.)

16 Now which three club ground names include the names of saints?

Answers on page 80

Badges

The aim here is to discover the identity of eight footballers. Study each group of club badges. Once you have identified them you should be able to find a player for each group who has been consecutively connected with each club.

To make it a more difficult quiz, first study (a) and (b) badges. Can you find the player from these? If not, move on to badge (c). If you still haven't guessed the identity of the mystery footballer try with badge (d). All four badges should give you the answer.

You can make this into a competition with a friend. The first person answers the odd numbered questions and the second the even numbers. See who wins the most points.

4

5

6

7

8

Answers on page 81

The 1976-7 season

Brush up your memory of the past season.

1 Liverpool were champions again. How many times have they won the First Division title?

2 Of all the promoted clubs, which was the first to celebrate their promotion?

3 Who scored both of Holland's goals when they beat England 2-0 at Wembley?

4 Which club won the FA Vase for the second time in succession?

5 Which famous Scottish club lost its place in the Premier Division?

6 Which club won the FA Challenge Trophy?

7 Which club, along with Hereford United, suffered relegation from the Second Division on the same day?

8 Who was the first player to reach the 30 goal mark in League matches?

9 Who refereed the 1977 European Cup Winners Cup Final between Hamburg and Anderlecht?

10 Who was booked for telling a referee where the penalty spot was?

11 Which clubs, apart from Liverpool, were top of Division 1 on a Saturday evening?

12 Who became manager of Chesterfield in October 1976?

13 Besides Chelsea and Wolves which was the only other club to lead the Second Division at any stage of the season?

14 Name the clubs involved in an 8-2 result.

15 Which Third Division side was relegated again at the end of the season after gaining promotion just a season earlier?

16 Which player went from Burnley to Leeds?

17 Which club relegated into the Fourth Division for 1976-7 was promoted again at the end of the season?

18 Which player went from Spurs to Norwich City?

19 Who was the Second Division's leading scorer with a total of 31 League, FA Cup and League Cup goals?

20 Who finished on 26 goals—three behind Malcolm McDonald and Andy Gray—in the First Division (League and Cup) scoring charts?

Answers on page 81

The Third Division

1 Which 1976-7 club's home ground is not even in the club's town? (If you need a further clue: it's also a fishing port.)

2 Which clubs were relegated into the Third Division for the 1976-7 season?

3 Which Third Division club reached the Semi-final of the 1975-6 FA Cup?

4 Name either of the two Third Division clubs to reach the fifth round of the 1976-7 FA Cup.

5 Who went from Rotherham United to Sunderland for £100,000 in 1970 and now plays for England?

6 A Third Division player was the League's top scorer in both 1974-5 and 1975-6. Who was he?

7 Which two Third Division clubs had a former Footballer of the Year as their manager during the 1976-7 season?

8 How many 1976-7 Third Division club names begin with the letter L?

9 Which club plays at Gigg Lane?

10 Of the 1976-7 Third Division clubs, which two clubs' *full* titles begin with and end with the same letter?

11 Which 1976-7 Third Division club has had to re-apply five times for re-election to the Football League whilst in the Fourth Division?

12 Which club, who played in the Third Division in 1976-7, beat Everton in the Final of the 1976-7 FA Youth Cup?

13 Name the club that reached the FA Cup Final in 1966 and was in the Third Division in 1976.

14 Which was the last Third Division club to reach the Football League Cup Final?

15 One to really test your memory. When did the Third Division first operate as a separate unit, after the old Third North and South Leagues were abandoned?

16 Who gained full England caps in 1976 whilst with a Third Division club?

17 Which is the only Third Division side to reach the quarter-finals of one of the three major European club trophies?

18 Lancashire clubs won the Third Division three times on the trot from 1973 to 1975. Who were the winning clubs and in which order did they win the Third Division?

19 Which club was relegated to the Third Division for 1976-7, then was immediately relegated into the Fourth for 1977-8?

20 Which was the last club to win the Football League Cup while in the Third Division?

Answers on page 82

The Fourth Division

1 Which club set a Fourth Division record by attaining 74 points in the 1975-6 season?

2 Which was the most northern Fourth Division club competing in the 1976-7 season?

3 Name three clubs in the Fourth Division in 1976-7 with names beginning with the letter C.

4 How many Fourth Division clubs in 1976-7 were situated in Devon?

5 In the season 1976-7 which two Fourth Division clubs had 'County' in their title?

6 Which Fourth Division clubs in 1976-7 had recently changed their names?

7 For which club did Kevin Keegan and Ray Clemence play before joining Liverpool?

8 Which 1976-7 Fourth Division club has the largest ground (measured in terms of having the largest record attendance)?

9 Which 1976-7 Fourth Division club has the smallest ground (measured in terms of having the smallest record attendance)?

10 Name the 1976-7 Fourth Division club ground on which International matches are often staged.

11 Which Fourth Division side reached the Football League Cup Final?

12 In 1959, Welsh International keeper Vic Rouse became the first Fourth Division International. For which club was he playing at the time?

13 From which club was Norwich City's Kevin Reeves transferred in 1976-7?

14 Which 1976-7 First Division side was one of the *original* Fourth Division members?

15 Roy Dwight, who scored a goal and broke his leg in the 1959 Cup Final, is the uncle of one of the Fourth Division more famous 'off the field' men. Who is he?

16 Which Fourth Division player gained full caps for Wales in 1976?

17 Which current Fourth Division club has won the Division championship twice since 1965?

18 Which club has applied for re-election to the Fourth Division seven times in recent seasons?

19 Which Fourth Division club was replaced by Cambridge United?

20 Which 1976-7 Fourth Division clubs have won the FA Cup?

Answers on page 82

Nicknames

Which Football League clubs have the following nicknames?

1 The Cobblers	14 The Cherries
2 The Canaries	15 The Bees
3 The Tykes	16 The Pirates
4 The Peacocks	17 The Seals
5 The Owls	18 The Quakers
6 The Rams	19 The Gills
7 The Blades	20 The Imps
8 The Stags	21 The Magpies
9 The Lions	22 The Dons
10 The Grecians	23 The Posh
11 The Gunners	24 The Biscuit Men
12 The Villains	25 The Saints
13 The Trotters	

Answers on page 83

Grounds mix and match

Can you match these clubs and their grounds?

Clubs	Grounds
1 Bury	Maine Road
2 Preston North End	Filbert Street
3 Coventry City	Gresty Road
4 Workington	Deepdale
5 Newport County	Roots Hall
6 Aberdeen	Ibrox Park
7 Queen's Park	Highfield Road
8 Lincoln City	Tynecastle Park
9 Crewe Alexandra	Fratton Park
10 Southampton	Carrow Road
11 Bolton Wanderers	Gigg Lane
12 Arsenal	Hampden Park
13 Cliftonville	Borough Park
14 Portsmouth	The Dell
15 Norwich City	Pittodrie
16 Manchester City	Highbury
17 Hearts	Somerton Park
18 Rangers	Sincil Bank
19 Leicester City	Solitude!
20 Southend	Burnden Park

Answers on page 83

Club quiz

Test your knowledge of the following clubs.

Hull City

1 In which year was the team founded?
2 From 1960 to 1971 he scored 195 League goals before moving to Coventry City. Who is he?
3 Who is their current (1977) manager?
4 Their most capped player is now manager of a London club. Who is he?
5 Who did they sell for £200,000 in 1974?
6 What is the name of their ground?

Millwall

1 In which year was the club founded?
2 Between 1961 and 1974 he broke the club record for record appearances. Who is he?
3 Who is the most capped player in their history?
4 What is the name of their ground?
5 Which player did Millwall sell to Crystal Palace for £118,000 in 1973?
6 Who is the manager of the club?

Luton Town

1 In which year was Luton founded?
2 In which year did this club reach the FA Cup Final?
3 Which player was transferred in 1971 for £180,000?
4 What is the name of the club's ground?
5 What are the club's colours?
6 Who is Luton Town's manager?

Bristol Rovers

1 In which year were Rovers founded?
2 Who is the manager (1977)?
3 Who were 'Smash and Grab'?
4 For which clubs do 'Smash and Grab' play in 1977?
5 Who was Rovers' manager for 23 years during the 50s and 60s?
6 What is the name of their home ground?

Mansfield Town

1 Which was their year of foundation?

2 What is the name of their home ground?

3 How many times have the club won promotion to the Second Division?

4 Which player was sold for £50,000 to Middlesbrough in 1971?

5 Which famous former International used to manage the club?

6 In which county is Mansfield?

Oxford United

1 In which year was the club founded?

2 Who is the club's manager?

3 Which club did United replace in the Football League?

4 What is the name of the club's ground?

5 Who is the Welsh International defender who played for the club in the 1970s?

6 What was the name of the club in their Southern League days?

Answers on page 84

International Football

Next year the World Cup is with us again. Day after day, for something like three weeks, our television screens will be filled by the skills and artistry of the world's best players. But how much do you know about them?

If you watch *On the Ball* in *World of Sport* every Saturday lunchtime on ITV, you'll know that we like to keep you right up to date with football across the world.

And I find from my mail-bag that young football fans are keener than ever to learn more about the game and its players from Brazil to Belgium, from the United States to Yugoslavia.

I think you'll enjoy the World Cup section in this chapter and I hope you'll agree that our geography lesson is a little easier to take than the ones you get in the schoolroom!

The section on famous teams is something quite new. We've left out the names of three players from nine famous teams of the last decade. Your job is to fill in the blank spaces on those team sheets—and I doubt if any of you will manage it! Now that's a challenge you can't refuse!

Brian Moore

World stars on the move

Below is a list of ten famous Internationals who played outside their own country in the 1976-7 season. Can you give (a) the player's nationality, (b) the country in which he now plays and (c) his present club.

1 Johan Neeskens
2 Johnny Rep
3 Rob Rensenbrink
4 Branko Oblak
5 Mario Kempes
6 Ognan Petrovic
7 Enver Maric
8 Robert Gadocha
9 Henning Jensen
10 Woldimierz Lubanski

Answers on page 84

Famous teams

Below are some of the more famous team line-ups of the past few years, but three names are missing from each team. Find the missing names, and then see how good your friends are at naming them.

1 Southampton's 1976 FA Cup winning team was

1	Turner	7	?
2	Rodrigues	8	Channon
3	Peach	9	Osgood
4	Holmes	10	?
5	Blyth	11	Stokes
6	?		

2 Sunderland's 1973 FA Cup winning team was

1	Montgomery	7	Kerr
2	Malone	8	Hughes
3	Guthrie	9	Halom
4	?	10	Porterfield
5	Watson	11	?
6	?		

3 The West German winning 1974 World Cup team was

1	Maier	7	?
2	Vogts	8	Hoeness
3	?	9	Muller
4	Schwarzenbeck	10	Overath
5	Beckenbauer	11	Holzenbien
6	?		

4 The England 1973 team that drew 1-1 with Poland and
   so failed to qualify for the World Cup was

   1 Shilton   7 ?
   2 ?   8 Channon
   3 Hughes   9 Chivers
   4 Bell   10 Clarke
   5 McFarland   11 Peters
   6 Hunter   16 Sub?

These are more difficult to find

5 Celtic's 1967 European Cup winning side was

   1 Simpson   7 Johnstone
   2 ?   8 Wallace
   3 Gemmell   9 Chalmers
   4 Murdoch   10 ?
   5 McNeill   11 Lennox
   6 ?

6 Chelsea's 1971 European Cup Winner's Cup team who
   were 2-1 winners in the replay against Real Madrid. (In
   the first game Hollins played and Baldwin was
   omitted.)

   1 Bonetti   7 ?
   2 ?   8 Baldwin
   3 Harris   9 Osgood
   4 Cooke   10 Hudson
   5 ?   11 Houseman
   6 Webb   Sub Smethurst

7 Newcastle United's 1969 Fairs Cup team against Ujpest Dosza in the Final was

1	McFaul	7	Scott
2	Craig	8	?
3	Clark	9	Davies
4	Gibb	10	?
5	?	11	Sinclair
6	Moncur		Sub Foggon

8 Arsenal's 1970 FA Cup winning team in their double season was

1	Wilson	7	Armstrong
2	Rice	8	?
3	?	9	Radford
4	Storey	10	?
5	McLintock	11	George
6	Simpson		Sub Kelly

9 Manchester United's 1968 European Cup winning team was

1	Stepney	7	Best
2	?	8	?
3	Dunne	9	Charlton
4	Crerand	10	Sadler
5	Foulkes	11	?
6	Stiles		

Answers on page 85

Scotland

1 Which Scottish Second Division side is nicknamed 'The Bully Wee'?

2 Who plays at Palmerston Park?

3 Name the two brothers who are managers of Scottish Premier League sides.

4 Who won the Scottish League Cup in 1976-7?

5 Which is Scotland's most southern Football League club?

6 Which two clubs won promotion from the Scottish Second Division in the 1976-7 season?

7 Who knocked Rangers out of the European Cup in the 1976-7 season?

8 Name three Scottish clubs Joe Harper has played for.

9 Who did Rangers beat in the 1975-6 Scottish Cup Final?

10 Which famous ex-Celtic player is now manager of Aberdeen?

11 In which town would you find Albion Rovers?

12 Who scored the winning goal in the 1976-7 Scottish Cup Final?

13 Which club changed its name from Ferranti Thistle in 1974 so that it could join the Scottish League?

14 Who is the 1976-7 Scottish Footballer of the Year?

15 In which League would you find Brora Rangers, Elgin City, Deveronvale and Forres Mechanic?

Answers on page 85

Wales and Ireland

1 He won 57 caps for Wales, was a famous member of the great Spurs team of the 1960s, and is one of only two Welshmen so far to win more than 50 caps. Who is he?

2 Which former Welsh International now manages Shrewsbury Town?

3 Which is the oldest League club in Wales?

4 He played for Wales several times up to 1974. Another clue is that his surname is the same as another sport. Who is he?

5 Who scored for Wales, on his debut, in the 1976 centenary match with England?

6 Southampton played an Irish Second Division club in the second round of the 1976-7 European Cup Winners Cup. Name the club.

7 For which Irish club did George Best play a few games in 1975-6?

8 For which club does Irish International, Derek Spence, now play?

9 Who, up to 1977, was the last Eire International to win an FA Cup Winners medal?

10 Whose record number of Eire International caps did Johnny Giles beat, with his 48th cap in 1977?

11 Who is the only player in Wales and Ireland to cost a £300,000 transfer fee?

12 Who were Wales's representatives in the 1976-7 European Cup Winners Cup?

13 Which club won the 1976-7 Welsh Cup?

14 What was the result of England v Wales qualifying match at Wembley in the 1974 World Cup?

15 Who was the former Welsh International who played for Team America against England in 1976?

16 Which Welsh non-League clubs have represented their country in European competitions?

17 Which club won the First Division of the League of Ireland in 1976-7 (a club far away from the established centres)?

18 Who were three Irishmen to win FA Cup winners medals at Wembley in 1977?

19 Who were the two Irish Internationals who failed to make the Manchester United team for the 1977 Cup Final, yet played for Northern Ireland seven days later in the Home International Championships?

20 What was the name of the ground where Eire beat France 1- 0 in a 1977 World Cup qualifying match?

Answers on page 85

A geography lesson

You probably know all these famous European clubs but can you match them up with cities which we show you on this map of Europe? Some cities have two clubs in the following list.

1 Grasshoppers
2 Feyenoord
3 Fenerbache
4 Lazio
5 Benfica
6 Ajax
7 Servette

8 Anderlecht
9 Espanol
10 Juventus
11 Schalke 04
12 Ujpest
13 Panathinaikos
14 Partisan

15 Standard
16 Racing White
17 Honved
18 Boavista
19 Beerschot

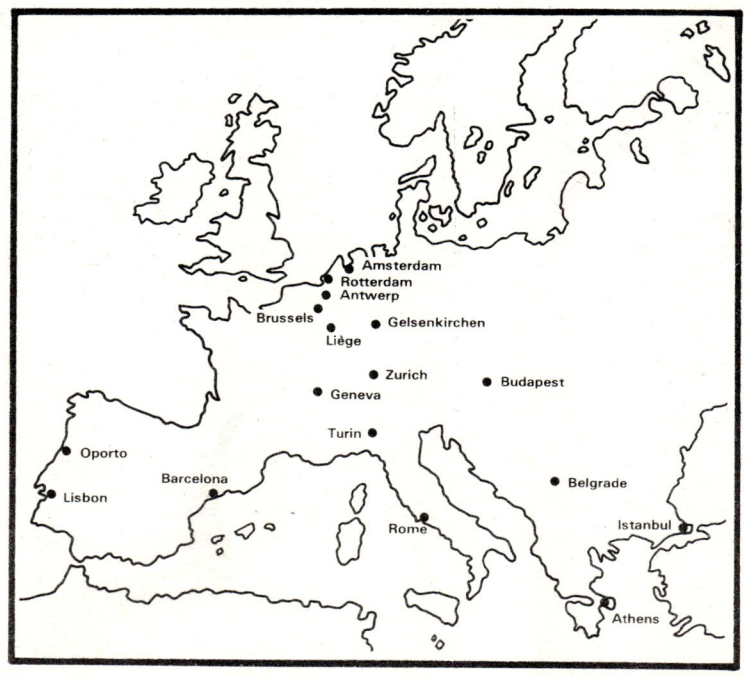

Answers on page 86

Europe

1 In the mid-1970s which Russian club was also Russia's National side?

2 There are an increasing number of British players joining foreign clubs. For which foreign club did the following play in 1976-7?

   a) Nick Deacy   d) Martin Chivers
   b) Roger Davies   e) Duncan McKenzie
   c) Peter Anderson   f) Ray Clarke

3 When the Dutch came to Wembley in 1977, the skills of Cruyff, Neeskens and company demoralized England. Who was their manager?

4 Who was the Dutch keeper in this match?

5 Who were the teams in the only all English EUFA Cup Final?

6 All the clubs below were champions of their country in 1976, and qualified for the 1976-7 European Cup. Which countries do they represent?

   a) St Etienne   d) Partisan
   b) Steaua   e) Jeunesse d'Esch
   c) Banik Ostrava

7 Name 6 major European First Division club sides, other than Dynamo Kiev, with the word 'Dynamo' in their title.

8 Who scored Czechoslovakia's winning penalty in the 1976 European Football Championship Final?

9 Who in the same match missed West Germany's penalty?

10 Who was elected European Footballer of the Year in 1975?

Answers on page 86

European cups

To get into Europe is a manager's main aim. Test your knowledge about European matches.

1 Which of the three major European club trophies up to 1977 had never been won twice in a row by any one club?

2 Anderlecht beat West Ham in the 1976 European Cup Winners Cup Final. Which English Football League club defeated Anderlecht in their earlier appearance in a European final?

3 Which is the only Football League club (other than Liverpool) to have won two of the major European club trophies?

4 Which two Football League clubs have won the EUFA Fairs Cup twice?

5 Which East German team won one of the three major European club trophies in 1974?

6 The most recent European Cup Final to be played at Wembley took place in 1971. Who won the match?

7 A European Cup attendance record was set up in 1970. Leeds was one of the clubs involved. Which club did they play?

8 Which Football League club beat Jeunesse Hautcharange 21-0 on aggregate in the 1971-2 European Cup Winners Cup?

9 Which German club lost in the 1973 EUFA Cup Final before going on to win the same trophy in 1975?

10 How many Football League sides have Anderlecht beaten in the European Cup Winners Cup tournaments of 1975-6 and 1976-7?

11 Which was the last English club to represent the Football League as the losing Cup finalist in the Cup Winners Cup?

12 Which other European countries besides England may currently put forward four representatives for the EUFA Cup?

13 Which was the first Dutch team to win the European Cup?

14 Which two clubs have won both the European Cup and the European Cup Winners Cup?

15 On their way to victory in the 1977 European Cup, Liverpool lost two away games. Who beat them?

16 Which two Football League clubs have, including 1977, made most appearances in the European Cup?

17 Which famous player scored a hat trick in a European Cup Final, yet finished on the losing side?

18 Which is the only Iron Curtain club to reach the European Cup Final?

19 The Football League had a marvellous record of successes in the Fairs/EUFA Cup between 1968 and 1973. Give the winners for the following years: 1967-8, 1968-9, 1969-70, 1970-1, 1971-2, 1972-3.

20 Who scored Borussia Munchen Gladbach's goal in the 1977 European Cup Final?

Answers on page 86

World Cup

1974

1 Which of these 1974 Dutch players did not play for Ajax at the time of the World Cup Final—Rep, Rensenbrink, Haan, or Krol?

2 Who were the two goalkeepers in the 1974 World Cup Final?

3 Which country, besides Brazil and Yugoslavia, was in Scotland's 1974 World Cup qualifying group?

4 Who was the top scorer in the final stages of the 1974 World Cup?

5 Name either of the two sets of Brazilian players who had the same surname but were not related.

1970

1 Roumania and Czechoslovakia were England's opponents in the 1970 World Cup Final group matches in Mexico. Which was the fourth team in the group?

2 Uwe Seeler and Gerd Muller scored a goal each against England in the quarter final. Who scored the other goal?

3 Who was captain of the 1970 World Cup winning team?

4 Which little country won its way through to the final stages despite going to war for six days as a result of a qualifying match?

5 Who scored Italy's goal in the final?

1978

1 What is the name of the stadium where the 1978 World Cup Final will take place?

2 Which two countries are automatic qualifiers?

3 Name any two of the four cities outside Buenos Aires where matches will take place.

4 To qualify for the final stages, which country will Scotland and Wales have to beat?

5 Which South American country has failed to make the Finals for only the second time ever, 1958 being the other occasion?

6 At which other sport is Argentina rapidly improving? Their progress is reflected in a one point loss in Cardiff.

7 What is the Libertadores Cup?

8 Which European country has to play off with a South American country before making the Finals?

9 Can you name three of Argentina's best clubs?

10 When was the last time that the World Cup was held in South America?

Answers on page 87

Mixed Bag

We call this a Mixed Bag—and that is exactly what it is. I think you'll enjoy the True or False section, but it is probably the Free For All questions that will puzzle you most. It amazed me, for example, to find that five Derby County players—as of the summer of 1977—had surnames that were also first names. Try that one on your friends at school tomorrow!

You might find the history of a sport a little dry and dusty in contrast to the colour and drama in the modern game. But the section on football's history is done in a way to entertain you—with three or four choices that might help to point you in the right direction.

Incidentally, I warned you at the start of the book that we should be giving the experts among you the chance to test your football knowledge. Now it is your turn with our So You Think You Are An Expert section. Twenty high-powered questions—and if you get even ten correct you will have done well. See if Dad or big brother can do better!

Mixed bag

1 Where were the 1972 Olympic Finals staged?

2 Who scored nine goals in an FA Cup tie in the 1970s?

3 Who scored five goals in a match for England in 1975?

4 Which Irishman scored four goals for his country in a 1975 international match?

5 Gordon Banks and Pat Jennings have both been Footballers of the Year, but which of the two was Footballer of the Year in 1973?

6 Which club won a 1973-4 Football League championship by 15 points?

7 Which club played in the First Division in 1972 and in the Fourth Division in 1975?

8 Which county won all four Divisions of the Football League in 1972-3?

9 A firm withdrew from sponsoring its own cup in 1975. Which cup was it?

10 Which club won both the 1971 and 1973 League Cup Finals at Wembley?

11 Which is the most southern First Division (1976-7) club?

12 Which footballers played cricket in 1976 for the counties listed below?

   a) Worcestershire (3 players)

   b) Leicestershire (2 players)

   c) Yorkshire (1 player)

13 Which recent England International has a surname which, minus the letter E, is the same as another sport?

14 For which clubs did these tongue-twisting names play in 1976-7?

   a) Anton Otulakowski
   b) John Ruggiero
   c) John Chiedozie
   d) Tunji Banjo
   e) Mike Czuczman
   f) Manny Andruszewski
   g) Rachid Harkouk

Answers on page 88

True or false

1 West Germany are the reigning Olympic soccer champions.
2 Luxembourg was in England's World Cup qualifying group in the 1960s.
3 The same club knocked both Manchester United and Manchester City out of the 1976-7 EUFA Cup.
4 Franz Beckenbauer gained his 100th cap in the 1976 European Football Championship Semi-Final.
5 Pat Jennings is currently (1977) Northern Ireland's second most capped footballer.
6 Everton bought the Football League's first £300,000 footballer.
7 Danny Blanchflower was the first player to be elected Footballer of the Year twice when he was elected a second time in 1961.
8 Carlisle United is geographically the English Football League's most northern club.
9 Austria was the second foreign country to beat England at Wembley.

10 Sepp Maier was West Germany's goalkeeper in the 1966 World Cup Final.

11 The first substitute in a Football League match was used in 1965.

12 Joe Mercer was the last man to have both played in, and managed, Football League championship winning teams.

13 Tom Finney has scored more goals for England than Geoff Hurst.

14 When England played West Germany in 1975, the visitors paraded a coloured centre forward.

15 Tony Waiters has played for England.

16 West Ham United beat Bayern Munich in the European Cup Winners Cup Final.

17 Spurs have won the FA Cup more times than Manchester United.

18 Milijia Aleksic is Yugoslavia's keeper.

19 QPR have had 12 home grounds.

20 Jimmy Greaves scored all his League goals in the First Division.

21 A man called Wilson has played for Italy.

22 Stan Mortensen scored the last (1977) Wembley Cup Final penalty.

23 Slovan Bratislava are the Czechoslovakian army side.

24 There are five clubs in Scotland beginning with the letter A—Ayr United, Albion Rovers, Aberdeen, Aidrieonians and Alloa Athletic.

25 Blackpool were the last team to score 4 goals in a Wembley FA Cup Final.

Answers on page 88

For the experts

All these clubs played in the First Divisions of their respective European Leagues in 1976-7, though are less known than the regular champions. Which countries do they belong to?

1 Go ahead Eagles, Deventer
2 Beveren Waas
3 VFL Bochum
4 Varzim
5 Kavala
6 Admira Wacker
7 University of Craiova
8 Skoda Pilzen
9 Velez Mostar
10 Valanciennes
11 Red Boys Differdange
12 Raba Eto
13 Karl Marx Stadt
14 Chacter Donetz
15 Hercules Alicante

Answers on page 89

Penalties

It's amazing to recall how penalty awards have altered the fate of matches. Below are some of the more famous incidents of the last few years.

1 Who scored the equalizing penalty in the 1974 World Cup Final and for which club does he now play?
2 Whose last minute penalty in the Semi-Final of the 1971 FA Cup saved the match for Arsenal and allowed them to continue their bid for the Double?
3 Who saved two penalties in one match at Anfield?
4 Who slotted home the rebound after having his penalty saved in a Cup Final in 1975?
5 Who scored a penalty in the 1977 European Cup Final?
6 Whose miss cost Queen's Park Rangers a semi-final place in the 1976-7 EUFA Cup?
7 Who scored from the spot in the Semi-Final of the 1976 FA Cup?

8 England's only goal in the 1973 match against Poland was also scored from the spot. Who was the scorer?

9 The turning point in the 1976 European Cup Winners Cup Final was a penalty given against West Ham United. Who scored to make it 3-2 to Anderlecht?

10 Similarly, the first goal in the 1977 European Cup Winners Cup Final was also a penalty. Who scored that one?

Answers on page 89

Free for all

1 Name five Derby County players who have surnames that are first names or Christian names?

2 Which First Division club has two keepers on its books who have surnames that are often first names? And who are the keepers?

3 Name players from each of the following clubs whose surnames are first names: Arsenal, Sunderland, Everton and Queen's Park Rangers.

4 Who are the three Liverpool players who surnames are also first names?

5 Among Liverpool's players there is one who has the same surname as a Prime Minister, and two who have surnames of recent American presidents. Who are they?

6 On the subject of Presidents, which Second Division club has a player whose surname is the same as that of the current American President?

7 Which 1976-7 First Division club often changed its colours from blue to green?

8 Which First Division player has the same surname as the singer of 'Somewhere over the Rainbow'?

9 Which ex-Arsenal and QPR player has the same surname as a famous composer?

10 Which two London grounds can also be found on Underground maps?

11 One for the historians. The battle that King Harold fought before the Battle of Hastings is the same as the name of a London ground. Which battle and which club?

12 Which club plays its home matches at Plough Lane?

13 There are many Taylors playing football—how many can you name? (There are seven in the 1976-7 First and Second Division.)

Answers on page 89

Football history

Here are some more early facts. After each question are four possible answers—can you guess which one is correct? If you feel confident you can try answering the questions without looking at the possible answers.

1 What did Sam Widdowson introduce to soccer in 1874?
   a) shinguards   b) numbers on shirts   c) shorts above the knee   d) a referee's whistle

2 England's first defeat on foreign soil was in 1929. Which country was the opposition?
   a) France   b) Spain   c) Holland   d) Belgium

3 Who was England's first full International substitute?
   a) Alan Ball   b) Martin Peters   c) Jackie Milburn   d) Jimmy Mullen

4 Portsmouth and Newcastle United took part in the first Football League match under floodlights. In which year?

a) 1936   b) 1946   c) 1956   d) 1966

5 Alf Common was, back in 1905, the first player to be transferred for £1,000. He went from Sunderland to where?

a) Middlesbrough b) Newcastle United c) Manchester United   d) Arsenal

6 Which club, in 1925-6, had no fewer than 17 full Internationals on its books?

a) Arsenal   b) Cardiff City   c) Celtic   d) Coleraine (Ireland)

7 Which was the first football club to form itself into a limited company?

a) Wolverhampton Wanderers   b) Birmingham City c) Aston Villa   d) West Bromwich Albion

8 Joe Payne, in 1936, scored 10 goals in a Football League match, a record. Payne played for

a) Norwich City   b) Ipswich Town   c) Coventry City d) Luton Town

9 The highest number of goals scored in a First Division season is 128 in 1930-1. Which club scored them?

a) Aston Villa   b) Tottenham Hotspur   c) Preston North End   d) Leeds United

10 A club has twice conceded just 24 goals in a First Division season. Which one was it?

a) Leeds United   b) Manchester United   c) Liverpool d) Arsenal

Answers on page 90

Rules of the game

1 A player wears an ornamental ring, which the referee considers to be dangerous. May the referee take any action?

2 In extreme inclement weather conditions, may players wear tracksuit trousers?

3 Are balls in two or more colours permitted in competitive football in this country?

4 If a defender intentionally trips an opponent on the penalty area line, what action should the referee take?

5 May a player lean on the shoulder of a team mate in order to gain height to head the ball?

6 When is a ball out of play?

7 Has a captain of a team the right to question the referee politely concerning his decision?

8 If a referee inadvertently blows his whistle for time at the end of the first half when there are still five minutes to play, may he add this on at the end of the match, or should he play five minutes short in the second half of the match?

9 At the taking of a throw-in, is it an offence to have part of a foot inside the field of play?

10 It is necessary, in all cases except one, for opposing players to be at least 10 yards from the ball at the taking of a free kick. What is the one case where this is not necessary?

11 If a player is sent from the field of play for serious misconduct, prior to the start of the match, may he be replaced?

12 What seven items must a referee take on to a field of play?

Answers on page 90

Soccer dates

Below is a list of dates of recent matches, and their venues. Which games were they, who were the teams playing, and what were the scores?

1 16th March, 1977 at Hillsborough
2 5th May, 1976 at Brussels
3 17th November, 1976 at Rome
4 14th June, 1970 at Leon
5 7th July, 1974 at Munich
6 28th May, 1975 at Paris
7 24th May, 1975 at Wembley
8 17th October, 1973 at Wembley
9 30th October, 1975 at Bratislava
10 24th March, 1976 at Wrexham

Answers on page 91

Some early dates

On the left hand side is a number and an event, and in the right hand column is a letter and a date. Can you match the events with the years in which they took place?

1	First World Cup	a) 1954
2	First Footballer of the Year award	b) 1963
3	First Football League substitute goal scorer	c) 1930
4	Wolves champions for the first time	d) 1948
5	First Wembley Football League Final	e) 1967
6	First England cap for Gordon Banks	f) 1965

And another six

1	FA XI play in the Charity Cup Final	a) 1966
2	First European Cup	b) 1963
3	England field 7 Arsenal players	c) 1965
4	Blackpool win the F.A. Cup	d) 1961
5	First international £100,000 Football League transfer	e) 1955
6	First cap for Jack Charlton	f) 1934

Answers on page 91

So you think you're an expert?

1 Name the two clubs that have played in all four Divisions of the Football League, and the old Third Divisions North and South?

2 Who was the Chelsea player called on as substitute in both the 1970 FA Cup Final and its replay?

3 Who is the most recent player to have scored 100 League goals for *two* different clubs?

4 Of which Football League club was Sir Stanley Matthews manager?

5 At which ground in 1974 did the first Sunday Football League match take place?

6 Which British soccer teams compete for the Murratti Vase?

7 Who scored America's Bicentennial goal against England in 1976?

8 Which was the first third from bottom club to be relegated to the Second Division under the rewritten promotion and relegation laws?

9 Who was the first player to represent England at all levels—Schools, Youth, Amateur, Under-23 and full International?

10 Before Celtic recorded their nine consecutive Scottish League wins, which club won the Scottish League in 1964-5?

11 Who is the player who played in the first ever European Cup Winners Cup Final in 1960-1 and is still playing First Division football in 1977?

12 Two West Germans played in the 1973 European Cup Final. Who were they?

13 Who is the only player to have scored a goal in three finals: (a) that of the Football League Cup, (b) of an FA Cup Final, and (c) of one of the three major club European cup competitions?

14 Which was the first club to come through from the Third Division to win the First Division championship?

15 Ronnie Corbett has a cousin who played for Scotland and Hearts as an inside forward around the time of the 1958 World Cup. Who is he?

16 Who, before Phil Neal in 1977, was the last man to score a penalty in a European Cup Final and what other record does the same man hold in the competition?

17 Which country had representatives in all three European Cup Finals in 1962?

18 Which club lost just one League match in the whole of the 1976-7 season yet failed to win its League title?

19 Which three West German players, who played in the World Cup Final of 1966, were all with the same club at that time?

20 Which club finished sixth in Division 2 in 1914-15 and was promoted in 1919?

Answers on page 92

Pot pourri—1

1 Who was Rangers' manager in 1975-6 when they won the Scottish League?

2 In the 1974 World Cup whom did Poland beat in the Third Place Play-off?

3 Which American club did George Best leave to join Fulham?

4 Which famous trophy has been replaced by the FA Challenge Vase?

5 Which Brazilian played 111 times for this country?

6 Which Football League club wear tangerine shirts as their first strip?

7 Which cup has been won by Chester, Bristol City, South Liverpool and Shrewsbury among others?

8 How many Englishmen have played 100 times for their country and who are they?

9 Which Englishman did Joao Havelange replace as President of FIFA?

10 Which former Welsh International now masterminds the US soccer scene?

11 Which country provides a team for only one of the three major European club cups?

12 Which was Emlyn Hughes' first League club?

13 Which First Division keeper was born in Calcutta?

14 Name four clubs who, since 1970, have spent just one season in the First Division before being relegated again.

15 There are two Borussia's in the West German First Division. Borussia Munchen Gladbach and Borussia Dortmund. What does Borussia mean?

16 In which country is Malcolm Allison an advisory with Galatassary?

17 The last First Division side to score 100 League goals did so in 1962-3. Which club achieved that feat?

18 Which First Division club played Barcelona in 1971 to decide permanent possession of the Fairs Cup?

19 Prior to 1977, when was the last time that Manchester United won the FA Cup?

20 Who first led Oxford United to promotion as a player, and then as a manager did the same in 1977 with another university town club, Cambridge United?

Answers on page 92

Pot pourri—2

1 With which country do you associate all the following players? Svehlik, Capkovic, Pivornik and Vencel

2 Which is the only London Football League side never to have played in the First Division?

3 For which club did Johan Cruyff play in 1976-7?

4 Which Irish club did Liverpool beat in the first round of the 1976-7 European Cup?

5 What does the word 'Bayern' in the club title, Bayern Munich, mean?

6 In 1972 which club made way for Hereford United to join the Football League?

7 Which Football League club is reputed to have the largest pitch in area?

8 Which country was captained by Paatelainen in a World Cup qualifying match at Wembley in 1977?

9 Which Football League club plays its home matches at Boundary Park?

10 Which Football League club did Dave Mackay manage before managing Derby County?

11 After Bristol City had bought Chris Garland for £100,000, which 1976-7 First Division club was the only First Division club not to have bought a player for that sum?

12 Howard Kendall is, currently, the youngest player to have appeared in a Cup Final. For which club was he playing at the time?

13 Which other London ground, besides Wembley, staged a match in the World Cup final stages of 1966?

14 Where did the replayed FA Cup Final of 1970 take place?

15 Manchester United 4 Benfica 1 was an historic scoreline. Who scored the United goals on the night they won the European Cup?

16 Which country is scheduled to host the 1982 World Cup?

17 The Bayern Munich manager, who led his team to triumph in the European Cup finals of 1974 and 1975, also led the Borussia Moenchen Gladbach to the 1977 final. Who is he?

18 Between playing for Millwall and Manchester United, Alex Stepney played one League game for another League club. Which club was it?

19 Which non-League club gained nationwide fame by going through their 1976-7 League programme unbeaten, until falling at the very last hurdle losing 3-1 to Barry Town in their last League game?

20 Which club has accumulated most points during their entire First Division existence?

Answers on page 93

Pot pourri—3

1 Which player first followed Jack Charlton to Middlesbrough from Leeds?

2 Which two clubs won the League Championship in 1973 and 1974 in between Derby County's two successes in 1972 and 1975?

3 Who were the managers of the 1974 FA Cup finalists?

4 Ted McDougall first signed for Liverpool. Which six clubs has he played for since?

5 Which was Allan Birchenall's first League club?

6 In which town are the offices of the Football Association of Wales?

7 Who scored England's first goal in the qualifying stages towards the 1978 World Cup?

8 If Yeovil Town and Scarborough played at Wembley, which cup final would be at stake, assuming it's not the FA Cup Final?

9 Who is Italy's most capped footballer of all time?

10 Which was Mike Summerbee's first Football League club?

11 Who is the Football League's only uncapped £300,000 player?

12 What do European clubs, Bayern Munich, Hertha Berlin, Lazio, FC Amsterdam and AC Roma have to do with the Olympic Games?

13 Who was the only member of Chelsea's promotion winning staff of 1976-7 to cost £200,000?

14 Liverpool play at Anfield, but which Scottish club play an Annfield?

15 Since 1970 the lowest number of points needed to win the First Division was 53, but by which club?

16 Who are the permanent holders of the Jules Rimet Cup?

17 Not including the London clubs, how many League clubs are there in Essex?

18 Not including the London clubs, how many League clubs are there in Kent?

19 Which was Roy McFarland's first Football League club?

20 Before Jimmy Case, who was the last player to score a goal in an FA Cup Final, and yet finish on the losing side?

Answers on page 93

Referee's Decisions

A footballer's job is hard enough, but I often think that the referee's is harder. Yet we all think we can do the job better than most of them!

Now you have the chance to see what *you* would do in certain tricky situations if you were in the referee's shoes.

The crowd are shouting, 'What about it, ref?' So blow your whistle and get on with it!

And when you've had a good look at this section it's worth thinking a little harder about the laws of the game in general. There are plenty of booklets on the subject but there is none better than the one published by the F.A. called *The Referee's Quiz Book* by Reg Paine.

There's no doubt that the more you know about the laws of the game the more you'll enjoy watching and playing. And if your leaning is towards refereeing, you will find a local referees' society only too happy to set you on your way.

Be a referee—1

An attacking player has been deliberately tripped by a defender in the penalty area. The referee blows his whistle and points to the penalty spot. Several players run over to him, gesticulating wildly but the referee waves them away. The penalty taker places the ball on the spot while the referee walks to the goalkeeper to warn him not to move until the ball has been kicked. The referee blows his whistle for the kick to be taken, but before the ball is kicked, a defender moves into the penalty area. What action shall the referee take?

Answer on page 94

Be a referee—2

There are many club grounds, school grounds and grounds in public parks, where the goal consists of two uprights and a bar with no net attached to catch the ball. At one such ground, after a deliberate foul in the area, the referee awarded a penalty. The penalty taker carefully placed the ball and on the referee's whistle ran up to take the kick. His shot had the keeper going the wrong way and whistled past, but was foiled from going through the goal by a spectator, obviously one of the other side's supporters, who couldn't bear to see a goal scored against his team. What action shall the referee take?

Answer on page 94

Be a referee—3

A goalkeeper has been constantly saving fierce shots and facing corners taken by his opponents. The pressure is still on him as he takes a goal kick. His supporters cheer as he runs to kick the ball and in his nervous state he slips and miskicks the ball. He sees an opposing player coming towards him so he runs after the ball and kicks it again. The referee blows his whistle. What action will he take?

Answer on page 94

Match Reports

Now it's time for you to become a Football Detective with this section of Match Reports. In it, we have described four games but with a number of important facts left out. It's your job to fill in the blank spaces with the help of a few clues that we have left along the way.

This is another section where you can compete against a friend. Each take a sheet of paper, one of you read the report and each of you write down the missing facts and see who gets the most correct answers at the end of the story. You need a knowledge of club and international football, but when you have completed our four reports you can quite easily compile a few of your own to keep the competition going.

Match report—1

Here is a report of a football match played in 1976. From the clues in the report, find the teams and fill in the other blanks. If you want to test your friends as well, each take a Match Report and compare scores!

.... and ...., one of whom plays at the Goldstone Ground and the other at Fellows Park, were engaged in a close struggle on Saturday. This match was distinguished by a performance from the Goldstone Ground club's Welsh International, ..., who tormented the home fullback but little came of his stream of accurate centres. The few chances created were easily dealt with by the Eire International keeper of the Fellows Park club, ..., and the .... (the nickname of the Goldstone Ground club) will have to reassess their chances of promotion. Representatives from two other clubs, ..., whose nickname is 'The Baggies', and ...., whose nickname is 'The Eagles', left before the final whistle after failing to agree terms with the visitors for their 30-goal striker.

Answers on page 94

Match report—2

Fill in the blanks using the clues.

Gloom at Brisbane Road after Saturday's home defeat against a club which, in 1976, asked Yorkshire County Cricket Club to leave their soccer ground. The home club, ..., have played five of their last eight games at home, but have lacked finishing power since the departure to West Bromwich of winger, ... The visitors, who hope to tempt the fair-haired ex-Derby and Wolves International winger, ..., out of retirement, are placed in midtable. The Brisbane Road club have two crucial matches, one against the only team in the Football League to play in blue and white quartered shirts, ..., and the second against 'The Tigers', ... But it seems that the final match of the season, against the team from Edgar Street, ..., who less than 10 years ago were in the Southern League, will determine whether a healthy final position is reached. Referee ...., who refereed all three 1977 League Cup Final matches, will officiate in the last game.

Answers on page 94

Match report—3

Fill in the blank spaces using the clues.

THE HOME SIDE: . . . .
CLUES   Home Internationals are played at such places as Sarajevo

               The country staged a major 1976 Tournament

               Red Star are the country's most famous club
and

THE VISITORS: . . . .
CLUES   Home Internationals are played at the Nepstadium

               They have beaten England 7-1

               Tibor Nyilasi is this country's hope for the future

A draw was all the home side needed, but they had previously suffered a heavy defeat against the same visiting side in the World Cup of 19...

CLUES   Brazil's second World Cup victory

               The match was played in Chile

Both teams had had a disappointing time recently. The home country had lost 2-1 to Sweden, whose scorers were . . . . (he's played in Holland for PSV for 5 years) and keeper . . . . (he plays in the German Bundesliga) from the penalty spot.

The visitors had lost by the only goal of the match against Czechoslovakia, whose scorer was . . . . (the centre back from Slovan Bratislava).

The referee in both these matches was . . . . (who refereed the 1976 Cup Final) (a further clue: a Welshman).

Answers on page 95

Match report—4

Again fill in the blank spaces using the clues.

An international match between

> ....

CLUES   Home ground is the Prater Stadium
           Nat Lofthouse made his name here
           Rapid are the country's most famous club

> and

> ....

CLUES   Home Internationals are played at the Vassil
           Kevski Stadium
           The country is in a 1978 World Cup
           qualifying group with Eire and France
           Bonev is the most famous international
           player

This match was an important step in the latter country's attempt to reach the final stages of the European Football Championship which was formerly called the Nations' Cup or .... Cup. The result was a scoreless draw.

The referee .... (he refereed in the 1970 World Cup Final) (a further clue—he's an East German), might have awarded at least two penalties to the home side.

In an earlier international match between Belgium and Holland, the referee awarded three penalties, one of which was converted.

The penalties were taken by .... (Ajax's many times capped right back and Rudi Krol's partner) and .... (who scored from the spot in the 1974 World Cup Final). Belgium's penalty was taken by .... (the FC Bruges striker, who has played 35 times for his country).

Answers on page 95

Answers

Players

World stars

1	Berti Vogts	Borussia Munchen Gladbach
2	Hans Krankl	Rapid Vienna
3	Christian Piot	Standard Liege
4	Jan Peters	NEC Nijmegen
5	Hugo Gatti	Boca Juniors
6	Zico	Flamengo
7	Franz Beckenbauer	New York Cosmos
8	Pirri	Real Madrid
9	Ralf Edstroem	PSV Eindhoven
10	Sepp Maier	Bayern Munich
11	Marian Masny	Slovan Bratislava
12	Dominique Rocheteau	St Etienne
13	Jurgen Croy	Sachsenring Zwickau
14	Dimitros Papaioannou	AEK Athens
15	Gregoriz Lato	Stal Mielec
16	Dino Zoff	Juventus
17	Johan Cruyff	Barcelona
18	Rene Botteron	Zurich
19	Oleg Blokhine	Dynamo Kiev
20	Laszlo Balint	Ferencvaros

Who am I?

1 Arfon Griffiths 2 Bob Wilson 3 Jimmy Hill 4 Bobby Charlton 5 Alan Ball 6 Tommy Docherty

The name's the same

1 a) Billy Casper, the golfer and Frank Casper, who has scored many vital goals for Burnley b) Paul is Ipswich's keeper, and Henry Cooper, our best known boxer c) Joe Gallagher's surname is pronounced the same as Bernard Gallacher, the golfer d) Rupert (the driver) and Kevin (the footballer) Keegan e) Rodney Marsh f) Slightly mis-spelt again, Jim Parks, the cricketer and Phil of QPR g) John Richards of Wolves, and namesake Vivian of the West Indies h) Jack Dempsey the boxer, and John of Chelsea i) Eric McManus the Notts County keeper and Mick McManus j) Keith Edwards (Sheffield United) and Gareth, the Welsh International

2 a) John Aston b) Peter Morris c) Terry Austin d) Andy Ford e) Bill Bentley

3 a) Mark Nightingale b) Keith Peacock (the Football League's first sub) c) John Sparrow d) Dennis Peacock e) Malcolm Partridge f) Alan Starling g) Ian Robins h) John Peacock i) Barry Swallow

4 a) Gerry Sweeney (Bristol City) and Jim Cannon (Crystal Palace) b) Gerry Peyton (Fulham, ex-Burnley) c) Alan Ball (Southampton) and Mervyn Day (West Ham) d) Trevor Womble (Rotherham United)

5 Hull City (Malcolm Lord), Leicester City (Steve Earle), Orient (Gerry Queen), ex-Coventry City (Brian King) and Everton (Andy King), Bristol Rovers (Frankie Prince), Swindon (Jim Barron) and Gillingham (Graham Knight)

6 a) Pat Rice (Arsenal) and Tony Currie (Leeds United) b) David Peach (Southampton), Trevor Cherry (Leeds), Steve Grapes (Cardiff City) c) Paddy Roche (Manchester United), Geoff Pike (West Ham) and Geoff Salmons (Stoke City)

7 a) Paul Mariner b) Ron Abbott c) Gary Collier d) Terry Naylor e) Keith Barber f) Allan and Norman Hunter

g) Allan Clarke, and his brothers; Brian Clark (Newport County) h) Joe Cooke (Bradford) and Mike Cook (Colchester) i) Keiron Baker j) John Miller (Mansfield), Alistair Millar (Barnsley) and Keith Miller (Bournemouth) k) Paul and Terry Cooper l) Ian Turner (Southampton) m)Steve Potter n) Paul Gardner o) Ken Tiler (Brighton) and Dudley Tyler (Hereford and West Ham) p) Butler q) Mike Packer r) Norman (Portsmouth) and Steve Piper (Brighton) s) Bill Glazier t) Garner u) Draper v) John Farmer

Families

1 Graham and Ray Wilkins   2 Tony Waddington (Stoke) selected son Steve for the first team   3 Bruce and Neil Rioch   4 John Toshak and John Mahoney   5 Jimmy, who joined Brian Greenhoff at Manchester United 6 Patrick and Hervé Revelli (St Etienne)   7 Cyril (Spurs) and Peter (Wolves) Knowles   8 René and Willy Van der Kerkhof (PSV Eindhoven)   9 John Hollins (QPR) and Dave Hollins (Newcastle United, Mansfield)   10 Alan and Ron Harris (Chelsea)   11 Eddie and Frankie Gray of Leeds, Eddie coming on as a sub   12 Gren Millington (Chester) whose brother Tony played for Wales   13 Dave (Birmingham) and Bob (Everton) Latchford and brother Peter (Celtic)   14 Paul and Ron Futcher   15 John Bond picked his son Kevin as a sub for Norwich City 16 Hibbitt   17 Foster   18 Bobby and Jack Charlton 19 Denis and Leslie Compton   20 Steve Sherwood (for a considerable time at Chelsea) has a brother John, who was third in David Hemery's great race at Mexico City 21 Martin and Paul Hinshelwood   22 Mike and Steve Gattling

The letters game in England

1 Colin Viljeon (Ipswich)   2 Jimmy Rimmer and John Radford (Arsenal)   3 David Nish (Derby), Phil Neal (Liverpool) and Keith Newton (Everton)   4 David

Johnson (then at Ipswich) and Mick Jones (Leeds)
5 Mike Doyle (Manchester City) and Martin Dobson
(Everton) 6 Jeff Astle (WBA) 7 Ian Storey-Moore and
Tommy Smith (Liverpool) 8 Phil and Peter Thompson
(Liverpool) 9 Gerry (QPR) and Trevor Francis
(Birmingham City) 10 Colin Harvey (Everton) 11 Alan
Ball (when with Arsenal), Stan Bowles, Trevor Brooking,
Jeff Blockley (ex-Arsenal) and Peter Bonetti 12 John
Gidman and Charlie George 13 Alec Lindsay and Chris
Lawler (Liverpool), Frank Lampard is the third
14 Hughes, Hurst, Hunt, Hunter and Hudson
15 Tueart, Thomas and Taylor   16 None surprisingly!
17 Mike Pejic, Stuart Pearson, Martin Peters and Phil
Parkes 18 Steve Whitworth, Frank Worthington and
Keith Weller (Leicester City) 19 Kevin Keegan and Ray
Kennedy (Liverpool) 20 Malcolm MacDonald and Paul
Mariner

The letters game in Scotland, Wales, Northern Ireland and Eire

1 a) Jim Bone b) Jim Brown c) Kenny Burns d) George
Best e) Ronnie Blair

2 a) Ronnie Rees b) Gil Reece c) David (Hull City), Phil
(Portsmouth), John (Arsenal and Birmingham) d) Alan
Rough (Partick Thistle) e) Damien Richardson

3 a) Graham Souness b) Colin Stein c) David Smallman
d) Pat Sharkey e) Gary Sprake

4 a) Noel Campbell b) Jim Conway c) Eddie Colquohoun
d) Charlie Cooke e) Les Cartwright

Hot shots

1 Bryan Robson   2 John Hickton   3 Duncan McKenzie
(then at Notts Forest) 4 Francis Lee 5 Ted McDougall
(then at Bournemouth) 6 Billy Jennings 7 Brian Little
8 Alan Buckley 9 Jimmy Greaves 10 Kenny Dalglish

11 Roger Davies (Derby County)   12 Brian Clough (then with Middlesbrough) 13 Ron Moore (Tranmere Rovers)   14 Kevin Hector (around 280 at the end of the 1976-7 season—he scored some with Bradford)

Players' names and places

1 Alan Slough (Fulham)   2 Alan Sunderland (Wolves) 3   Colin Boulton (Derby County)   4 Joe Bolton (Sunderland)   5 David Bradford (West Bromwich)   6 Roy Burton (Oxford)   7 Hamilton (there are several) 8 Kevin Charlton (Hereford)   9 Kenny Stroud (Swindon)   10 Clint Boulton (Torquay) 11   Peter Wells   12 Pat Holland (West Ham) and Joe Jordan (Leeds)   13 Alan Devonshire (West Ham)   14 Trevor Ross

Teams

The final tables

1 Swansea City (92)   2 Chelsea   3 Workington Town 4 The champions, Mansfield Town   5 Southport   6 Derby County   7 Bradford City   8 Southport and Halifax 9 Workington Town (102)   10 London (Chelsea and Crystal Palace)

Grounds

1 Sunderland (Rover Park), West Ham (Upton Park), Everton (Goodison Park), Aston Villa (Villa Park), Middlesbrough (Ayresome Park), Newcastle United (St James Park) 2 Exeter City; Hartlepool 3 Northampton Town (Northants CCC) 4 Chesterfield and Aldershot 5 Burnley (Turf Moor), Rotherham (Millmoor), Torquay United (Plainmoor) 6 Ipswich Town   7 Derby County (Baseball Ground)   8 Shrewsbury

Town (Gay Meadow), Notts County (Meadow Lane) 9 Manchester City 10 Fulham 11 Oak(well), Barnsley, Elm Park, Reading, and Ash(ton) Gate, Bristol City 12 Griffin Park, Brentford 13 The Valley, Charlton Athletic and Valley Parade, Bradford (City) 14 Belle Vue, which is the home of Doncaster Rovers 15 Abbey Stadium (Cambridge United), Priest(field) Stadium (Gillingham), Vicarage Road (Watford), Dean Court (Bournemouth) 16 St James Park (you can find the clues elsewhere in the book!), St Andrews (Birmingham City)

Badges

1 Malcolm MacDonald (Fulham, Luton, Newcastle United, Arsenal) 2 Allan Clarke (Walsall, Fulham, Leicester, Leeds United) 3 David Webb (Orient, Southampton, Chelsea, QPR) 4 Bryan 'Pop' Robson (Newcastle United, West Ham, Sunderland, West Ham) 5 Chris Garland (Bristol City, Chelsea, Leicester, Bristol City) 6 John O'Hare (Sunderland, Derby County, Leeds United, Notts Forest) 7 Peter Rodrigues (Cardiff City, Leicester City, Sheffield Wednesday, Southampton) 8 Phil Boyer (Derby County, York City, Bournemouth, Norwich)

The 1976-7 season

1 10 2 Wolverhampton Wanderers (into Division 1) 3 Jan Peters 4 Billericay Town 5 Hearts 6 Scarborough Town 7 Plymouth Argyle 8 Peter Ward (Brighton) 9 Pat Partridge 10 Joe Corrigan (Manchester City) v Derby County 11 Ipswich, Aston Villa and Middlesbrough 12 Arthur Cox 13 Blackpool 14 Derby County (8) Tottenham Hotspur (2) 15 Northampton Town 16 Ray Hankin 17 Colchester United 18 Jimmy Neighbour 19 Neil Whatmore (Bolton) 20 Brian Little (Aston Villa)

The Third Division

1 Grimsby, who play in Cleethorpes 2 Portsmouth, Oxford United, York City 3 Crystal Palace who lost 2-0 to Southampton 4 Port Vale who lost 3-0 to Aston Villa and Chester who lost 1-0 to Wolves 5 Dave Watson (now Manchester City) 6 Dixie McNeil (Hereford United) 7 Walsall (Dave MacKay), Brighton (Alan Mullery) 8 Only Lincoln City 9 Bury 10 York City, Northampton Town 11 Lincoln City 12 Crystal Palace (who were of course promoted in 1977) 13 Sheffield Wednesday 14 Aston Villa (in 1971) 15 Back in 1958 for the 1958-9 season 16 Peter Taylor (Crystal Palace) 17 Wrexham 18 Bolton Wanderers (1972-3), Oldham Athletic (1973-4), Blackburn Rovers (1974-5) 19 York City 20 Swindon Town (in 1969 they beat Arsenal 3-1)

The Fourth Division

1 Lincoln City 2 Hartlepool (2 miles north of Workington) 3 Colchester United, Cambridge United, Crewe Alexandra 4 Exeter City and Torquay United 5 Newport County, Stockport County 6 AFC Bournemouth, who used to be called Bournemouth and Boscombe Athletic, Hartlepool (Hartlepool United) and Swansea City (formerly Town) 7 Scunthorpe United 8 Huddersfield Town (record crowd 67,000) 9 Cambridge United (record crowd 14,000) 10 Swansea City's ground is the Vetch Field 11 Rochdale (in 1962) 12 Crystal Palace 13 Bournemouth 14 Coventry City 15 Elton John (real name Reg Dwight) 16 Alan Curtis (Swansea City) 17 Doncaster Rovers 18 Hartlepool 19 Bradford 20 Bradford City (promoted for 1977-8) and Barnsley.

Nicknames

1 Northampton Town 2 Norwich City 3 Barnsley
4 Leeds United 5 Sheffield Wednesday 6 Derby
County 7 Sheffield United 8 Mansfield Town 9 Millwall 10 Exeter City 11 Arsenal 12 Aston Villa
13 Bolton 14 Bournemouth 15 Brentford 16 Bristol
Rovers 17 Chester 18 Darlington 19 Gillingham 20 Lincoln 21 Newcastle United and Notts
County 22 Oxford and Wimbledon 23 Peterborough
24 Reading 25 Southampton

Grounds mix and match

Clubs	Grounds
1 Bury	Gigg Lane
2 Preston North End	Deepdale
3 Coventry City	Highfield Road
4 Workington	Borough Park
5 Newport County	Somerton Park
6 Aberdeen	Pittodrie
7 Queens Park Rangers	Hampden Park
8 Lincoln City	Sincil Bank
9 Crewe Alexandra	Gresty Road
10 Southampton	The Dell
11 Bolton Wanderers	Burnden Park
12 Arsenal	Highbury
13 Cliftonville	Solitude!
14 Portsmouth	Fratton Park
15 Norwich City	Carrow Road
16 Manchester City	Maine Road
17 Hearts	Tynecastle Park
18 Rangers	Ibrox Park
19 Leicester City	Filbert Street
20 Southend	Roots Hall

Club quiz

Hull City

1 1904   2 Chris Chilton   3 John Kaye   4 Terry Neill
5 Stuart Pearson (to Manchester United)   6 Boothferry
Park

Millwall

1 1885   2 Harry Cripps   3 Eamonn Dunphy   4 The Den
(Cold Blow Lane)   5 Derek Possee   6 Gordon Jago

Luton Town

1 1885   2 1959   3 Malcolm McDonald (to Newcastle
United)   4 Kenilworth Road   5 Orange   6 Harry
Haslam

Bristol Rovers

1 1883   2 Don Megson   3 Bruce Bannister and Alan
Warboys   4 Bannister now plays for Plymouth and
Warboys for Fulham   5 Bert Tann   6 Eastville

Mansfield Town

1 1905   2 Field Mill   3 Once, in 1977   4 Stuart Boam
5 Raich Carter (also Charles Mitten)   6 Nottinghamshire

Oxford United

1 1896   2 Mick Brown   3 Accrington Stanley   4 Manor
Ground   5 David Roberts   6 Headington United

International Football

World stars on the move

1 *Neeksens* a) Dutch b) Spain c) Barcelona
2 *Rep* a) Dutch b) Spain c) Valencia
3 *Rensenbrink* a) Dutch b) Belgium c) Anderlecht

4 *Oblak* a) Yugoslav b) West Germany c) Bayern Munich
5 *Kempes* a) Argentinian b) Spain c) Valencia
6 *Petrovic* a) Yugoslav b) France c) Bastia
7 *Maric* a) Yugoslav b) West Germany c) Schalke
8 *Gadocha* a) Polish b) France c) Nantes
9 *Jensen* a) Danish b) Spain c) Real Madrid
10 *Lubanski* a) Polish b) Belgium c) Lokeren

Famous teams

1   6 Steele, 7 Gilchrist, 10 McCalliog
2   4 Horswill, 6 Pitt, 11 Tueart
3   3 Breitner, 6 Bonhof, 7 Grabowski
4   2 Madeley, 7 Currie, 16 Hector
5   2 Craig, 6 Clark, 10 Auld
6   2 Boyle, 5 Dempsey, 7 Weller
7   5 Burton, 8 Robson, 10 Arentoft
8   3 McNab, 8 Graham, 10 Kennedy
9   2 Brennan, 8 Kidd, 11 Aston

Scotland

1 Clyde   2 Queen of the South   3 Jim McLean (Dundee United) and Willie McLean (Motherwell)   4 Aberdeen 5 Stranraer, some 15 miles south of Queen of the South 6 Stirling Albion and Alloa Athletic   7 FC Zurich 8 Morton, Aberdeen and Hibs   9 Hearts (by 3-1)   10 Billy McNeill   11 Coatbridge   12 Andy Lynch   13 Meadow-bank Thistle   14 Danny McGrain   15 The Highland League

Wales and Ireland

1 Cliff Jones   2 Alan Durban   3 Wrexham   4 Trevor Hockey   5 Alan Curtis (Swansea City)   6 Carrick Rangers   7 Cork Celtic   8 Blackpool   9 Steve Heighway (Liverpool)   10 Alan Kelly (Preston)   11 Leighton James (Derby County)   12 Cardiff City   13 Shrewsbury

Town   14 1-1   15 Mike England   16 Bangor City and Borough United   17 Sligo Rovers   18 Sammy McIlroy, David McCreerey and Jimmy Nicholl   19 Tommy Jackson and Chris McGrath   20 Landsdowne Road, where Ireland play their Rugby matches

A geography lesson

1 Zurich   2 Rotterdam   3 Istanbul   4 Rome
5 Lisbon   6 Amsterdam   7 Geneva   8 Brussels   9 Barcelona   10 Turin   11 Gelsenkirchen   12 Budapest
13 Athens   14 Belgrade   15 Liège   16 Brussels
17 Budapest   18 Oporto   19 Antwerp

Europe

1 Dynamo Kiev   2 a) PSV Eindhoven b) FC Bruges c) Royal Antwerp d) Servette Geneva e) Anderlecht f) Sparta Rotterdam   3 Jan Zwartkruis   4 Piet Schrijvers 5 Wolves and Tottenham Hotspur in 1972   6 a) France b) Rumania c) Czechoslovakia d) Yugoslavia e) Luxembourg   7 Dynamo clubs at Moscow, Dresden, Berlin, Zagreb, Bucharest and Tiblisi   8 Antonin Panenka   9 Ulli Hoeness   10 Oleg Blokhine (Russia)

European cups

1 European Cup Winners Cup   2 Arsenal in 1970 3 Tottenham Hotspur   4 Liverpool (1973 and 1976) and Leeds United (1968 and 1971)   5 FC Magdeburg, who won the Cup Winners Cup   6 Ajax, who beat Panathinaikos 2-0   7 Celtic, the match was played at Hampden Park (134,000) (the attendance at the Real Madrid-Frankfurt match was 130,000)   8 Chelsea 9 Borussia Munchen Gladbach   10 Three (Wrexham and West Ham United in 1975-6, and Southampton in 1976-7)   11 Liverpool (in 1971-2 after Arsenal won the 'Double')   12 Two—West Germany and Italy

13 Feyenoord (in 1970) 14 AC Milan (European Cup in 1963, Cup Winners Cup in 1968. They won the European Cup again in 1969): Bayern Munich (Cup Winners Cup 1967, European Cup 1974-5-6) 15 Trabsonspor of Turkey and St Etienne (both 1-0) 16 Manchester United have made five appearances and will be joined by Liverpool who make their fifth appearance in 1977-8 17 Ferenc Puskas (in 1962 for Real Madrid in the 5-3 defeat by Benfica) 18 Partisan Belgrade 19 1967-8 Leeds United, 1968-9 Newcastle United, 1969-70 Arsenal, 1970-1 Leeds United, 1971-2 Tottenham Hotspur, 1972-3 Liverpool

World Cup

1974

1 Rob Rensenbrink, who played for Anderlecht 2 Jan Jongbloed (Holland) and Sepp Maier (West Germany) 3 Zaire 4 Lato of Poland 5 The Marinho's and the Paulo Cesar's.

1970

1 Brazil 2 Franz Beckenbauer 3 Carlos Alberto (Brazil) 4 El Salvador 5 Roberto Boninsegna

1978

1 River Plate stadium 2 Argentina, as hosts, and West Germany as the holders 3 Rosario, Mendoza, Cordoba and Mar del Plata 4 Czechoslovakia (the third team in the group) 5 Uruguay 6 Rugby Union (Wales only beat them 20-19 in 1976) 7 It's the South American equivalent of the European Cup 8 Hungary 9 Boca Juniors, Independiente, River Plate, Hurucan, Rosario Central, Estudiantes, Racing Club are the best known—most have played in the World Club Cup Final 10 1962 in Chile

Mixed Bag

Mixed bag

1 West Germany   2 Ted McDougall for Bournemouth in the 11-0 FA Cup win against Margate—1st round November 1971   3 Malcolm McDonald in the 5-0 win against Cyprus   4 Don Givens for Eire v Turkey 5 Jennings. Banks was the 1972 winner   6 Middlesbrough (Second Division)   7 Huddersfield Town   8 Lancashire with Liverpool (Division 1), Burnley (Division 2) Bolton (Division 3), and Southport (Division 4)   9 The Texaco Cup   10 Tottenham Hotspur   11 Bristol City—3 miles south of QPR's ground   12 a) Phil Neale (Lincoln City), Ted Hemsley (Sheffield United) and Jim Cumbes (Aston Villa) b) Chris Balderstone (Doncaster Rovers, now Queen of the South) and Graham Cross (Brighton) c) Arnie Sidebottom (Huddersfield)   13 Stan Bowles (QPR) 14 a) West Ham United b) Brighton c) Orient d) Orient, again e) Scunthorpe United f) Southampton g) Crystal Palace

True or false

1 *False—East* Germany won the 1976 title 2 *True*—Luxembourg was in England's qualifying group for the 1962 World Cup as well as in the 1978 World Cup 3 *True*—Juventus beat both clubs 4 *False*—He gained his 100th cap against Czechoslovakia in the Final 5 *False*—He has more Irish caps than any other player 6 *True*—Bob Latchford, in February 1974 7 *False*—Tom Finney was elected Footballer of the Year in 1954 and 1957 8 *False*—Carlise is 12 miles south of Newcastle 9 *False*—Sweden won 3-2 at Wembley in 1959, Austria won by the same score in 1965 10 *False*—The goalkeeper was Tilkowski 11 *True*— Keith Peacock (Charlton) 12 *False*—Dave MacKay was (Spurs and Derby), also Bob Paisley, to name a couple of

the more recent examples 13 *True*—30 to Hurst's 24 14 *True*—Erwin Kostedde (Offenbach) 15 *True*—5 caps in 1964-5 16 *False*—1860 Munich, not Bayern 17 *True*—5 to 4 18 *False*—He plays for Luton Town! 19 *True* —They also played one match on Arsenal's ground 20 *True*—For Spurs and Chelsea 21 *True*—His Christian name is Guiseppe, he was born in Darlington and he plays for Lazio and Italy 22 *False*—Mortensen didn't take one, Blanchflower was the last in 1962 23 *False*—Dukla Prague are the army side 24 *False*— There are six (Arbroath is the other one) 25 *True*—In 1953

For the experts

1 Holland 2 Belgium 3 West Germany 4 Portugal 5 Greece 6 Austria 7 Rumania 8 Czechoslovakia 9 Yugoslavia 10 France 11 Luxembourg 12 Hungary 13 East Germany 14 Russia 15 Spain

Penalties

1 Paul Breitner, who has just signed for Eintracht Brunswick 2 Peter Storey 3 Pat Jennings 4 Ray Graydon of Aston Villa in the 1975 League Cup Final 5 Phil Neal of Liverpool 6 David Webb's shot was saved by substitute keeper Christidis of AEK Athens 7 David Peach of Southampton (v Crystal Palace) 8 Allan Clark 9 Rob Rensenbrink 10 Georg Volkert of SV Hamburg

Free for all

1 Daniel, George, Hector, James and Thomas 2 Leeds United—Harvey and Stewart 3 Pat Howard and Trevor Ross (Arsenal), Bob Lee (Sunderland), Mike Bernard (Everton), Dave Thomas and Gerry Francis (QPR) 4 Sammy Lee, Alec Lindsay and Phil Neal 5 Ian

Callaghan, Ray Kennedy and David Johnson 6 Notts
County (Steve Carter) 7 West Bromwich Albion
8 Chris Garland 9 Terry Mancini 10 Upton Park
and Highbury 11 Stamford Bridge (Chelsea)
12 Wimbledon 13 Peter (Spurs), Alan and Tommy (West
Ham), Stuart (Bristol Rovers), Steve (Bolton Wanderers),
and Gordon and Royston Taylor (Blackburn)

Football history

1 a, 2 b, 3 d, 4 c, 5 a, 6 b, 7 b (as Small
Heath), 8 d, 9 a, 10 c

Rules of the game

1 If the referee considers that the article may constitute a
danger to other players, he can order him to remove it
2 The usual equipment of a player is a jersey or shirt,
shorts, stockings and footwear. Tracksuit or similar
trousers may, however, be worn.
3 Yes. There is nothing in the Laws of the Game
indicating the colours of footballs. Competition rules,
however, may place an embargo on certain types of
balls.
4 Provided that the ball is in play, a penalty kick should
be awarded. The Laws of the Game state that the space
within the inside areas of the field of play include the
width of the lines marking these areas.
5 No. This is considered to be ungentlemanly conduct,
and should be penalised by a caution and an indirect
free kick to the opposing side.
6 When it has wholly crossed the goal-line, or touch-line,
or when the game has been stopped by the referee.
7 No. A captain has no right to do this.
8 Neither. The referee, upon realising that he has cut
short the time of the first half, should take the players
back on the field to play the requisite number of
minutes.

9 No—providing that a part of each foot is on the touch line, or on the ground outside the touch line, at the moment of release of the ball, and no other breach of the law is occasioned.
10 If they are standing on their own goal line between the goal posts when an indirect free kick is being taken against them from within their own penalty area.
11 Yes, but only by a named substitute. The kick-off must not be delayed to allow the substitute to join his team.
12 Cards (red and yellow), coin, stop watch, whistle, note-pad, pencil, and ball.

Soccer dates

1 The replay of the League Cup Final (Aston Villa 1 Everton 1).
2 European Cup Winners Cup Final (West Ham 2 Anderlecht 4).
3 World Cup Qualifier (Italy 2 England 0).
4 World Cup (England 2 West Germany 3).
5 World Cup Final (West Germany 2 Holland 1).
6 European Cup Final (Bayern 2 Leeds United 0).
7 Home International (England 5 Scotland 1).
8 1974 World Cup Qualifying match (England 1 Poland 1).
9 European National Cup (Czechoslovakia 2 England 1).
10 Centenary International (Wales 1 England 2).

Some early dates

First quiz

1 c,   2 d,   3 f,   4 a,   5 e,   6 b

Second quiz

1 d,   2 e,   3 f,   4 b,   5 a,   6 c

So you think you're an expert?

1 Grimsby Town, Coventry City 2 Marvin Hinton
3 Kevin Hector (Bradford and Derby County) 4 Port
Vale 5 Millwall (v Fulham) 6 The Channel Islands
7 Stewart Scullion, (Watford and Sheffield United)
8 Southampton 9 Terry Venables (1964)
10 Kilmarnock 11 Enrico Albertosi of Fiorentina, now
of AC Milan 12 Horst Blankenburg of Ajax, and
Helmut Haller, who came on as a sub for Juventus
13 Peter Osgood (Chelsea) v Stoke in the 1972 League
Cup Final, v Real Madrid in the 1971 European Cup
Winners Cup Final, and in the 1970 Cup Final replay
v Leeds 14 Portsmouth 15 Jimmy Murray 16 Velibor
Vasovic of Ajax. He became in that match the first man
to play in the European Cup Final for two different clubs,
Ajax and Partisan Belgrade in 1966 17 Spain. Real
Madrid in the European Cup, Athletico Madrid in the
Cup Winners Cup and Valencia and Barcelona in the
Fairs Cup 18 Torino—their record of P30 W21 D8 L1
Goals 50-14 just failed to pip Juventus with a 30-23-5-2-
51-19 record by 51 points to 50 19 Hans Tilkowski, Siggi
Held and Lothar Emmerich all played for Borussia
Dortmund 20 Arsenal—for the first season after World
War I

Pot pourri—1

1 Jock Wallace 2 Brazil 3 Los Angeles Aztecs 4 FA
Amateur Cup 5 Pele 6 Blackpool 7 The Welsh
Cup 8 Three: Bobby Moore, Bobby Charlton, Billy
Wright 9 Sir Stanley Rous 10 Phil Woosnam
11 Wales 12 Blackpool 13 Kevin Keelan (Norwich
City) 14 Blackpool, Carlisle United, Luton Town and
Sunderland 15 It comes from the word Prussia—part
of old Germany 16 Turkey 17 Tottenham Hotspur
18 Leeds United. As the then current holders, they
played Barcelona, who were the first winners 19
1963 20 Oron Atkinson

Pot pourri—2

1 Czechoslovakia 2 Millwall 3 Barcelona 4 Crusaders
5 Bayern is the German name for the state of
Bavaria, of which Munich is the capital 6 Barrow
7 Doncaster Rovers (118yds by 79yds) 8 Finland
9 Oldham Athletic 10 Nottingham Forest
11 Middlesbrough—£72,000. Phil Boersma is, so far, their
most expensive buy 12 Preston North End 13 White
City 14 Old Trafford 15 Bobby Charlton (2), George
Best and Brian Kidd 16 Spain 17 Udo Lattek
18 Chelsea 19 Worcester City 20 Everton (some 280
points more than Aston Villa)

Pot pourri—3

1 Terry Cooper 2 Liverpool 1972-3 and Leeds United
1973-4 3 Bill Shankly (Liverpool) and Joe Harvey
(Newcastle) 4 York City, Bournemouth, Manchester
United, West Ham United, Norwich City,
Southampton 5 Sheffield United 6 Wrexham 7 Stuart
Pearson in the 4-1 win against Finland 8 The FA
Challenge Trophy 9 Giacinto Facchetti 10 Swindon
Town 11 Bob Latchford (Everton) 12 Their home
pitches are in the middle of Olympic stadia 13 David
Hay 14 Stirling Albion 15 Derby County (in 1974-5)
16 Brazil. They kept the trophy outright after winning
the World Cup for the third time 17 Two—Colchester
United and Southend United 18 One only,
Gillingham 19 Tranmere Rovers 20 Team mate, Steve
Heighway, who scored in the 1971 final, when Liverpool
lost 2-1 to Arsenal

Referee's Decisions

Be a referee—1

He shall allow the kick to be taken, and if a goal is scored, it shall be awarded. If a goal is not scored, and no other separate breach of law occasioned, the kick shall be retaken.

Be a referee—2

The kick shall be retaken.

Be a referee—3

If the ball did not leave the penalty area, when the goalkeeper played it a second time, the kick should be retaken. The player who encroached should be cautioned. goalkeeper played it a second time, an indirect free kick should be awarded against him for playing the ball twice.

Match report—1

Brighton play at the Goldstone Ground, Walsall at Fellows Park. The Welsh International is Peter O'Sullivan, and Mick Kearns is Walsall's keeper. Brighton's new nickname is 'The Seagulls'. The Baggies are West Bromwich and Crystal Palace's nickname is the Eagles.

Match report—2

The Brisbane Road club is Orient, and the club who told Yorkshire Cricket Club to leave Bramall Lane was Sheffield United. Laurie Cunningham went to West Bromwich. Alan Hinton is the ex-Derby and Wolves winger. Bristol Rovers play in blue and white quarters, the

Tigers are Hull City. Hereford United play at Edgar Street. The referee is Gordon Kew.

Match report—3

The match was between Yugoslavia and the visitors, Hungary. The World Cup was that of 1962. The Swedish International—Ralf Edstrom, and Ronnie Hellstrom the keeper. Czech International was Ondrus. Referee—Clive Thomas.

Match report—4

The match was between Austria and Bulgaria. The competition was formerly also called the Henri Delauney Cup after its founder. The referee was Rudi Glockner. Dutch right back—Wim Suurbier; other scorer: Johan Neeskens. Belgian striker: Raoul Lambert.